Date: 6/7/16

J 634 PET
Pettiford, Rebecca,
Fruits /

WAY TO GROW! GARDENING
FRUITS

by Rebecca Pettiford

pogo

Ideas for Parents and Teachers

Pogo Books let children practice reading informational text while introducing them to nonfiction features such as headings, labels, sidebars, maps, and diagrams, as well as a table of contents, glossary, and index.

Carefully leveled text with a strong photo match offers early fluent readers the support they need to succeed.

Before Reading

- "Walk" through the book and point out the various nonfiction features. Ask the student what purpose each feature serves.
- Look at the glossary together. Read and discuss the words.

Read the Book

- Have the child read the book independently.
- Invite him or her to list questions that arise from reading.

After Reading

- Discuss the child's questions. Talk about how he or she might find answers to those questions.
- Prompt the child to think more. Ask: What is your favorite fruit? Does it grow from a tree, a bush, or a vine? Have you ever grown it yourself?

Pogo Books are published by Jump!
5357 Penn Avenue South
Minneapolis, MN 55419
www.jumplibrary.com

Library of Congress Cataloging-in-Publication Data

Pettiford, Rebecca, author.
  Fruits / by Rebecca Pettiford.
    pages cm. – (Way to grow! Gardening)
  Includes index.
  ISBN 978-1-62031-232-2 (hardcover: alk. paper) –
  ISBN 978-1-62496-319-3 (ebook)
  1. Fruit–Juvenile literature. I. Title. II. Series: Pettiford, Rebecca. Way to grow! Gardening.
  SB357.2.P48 2015
  634–dc23
                                                    2015000277

Series Editor: Jenny Fretland VanVoorst
Series Designer: Anna Peterson
Photo Researcher: Anna Peterson

Photo Credits: All photos by Shutterstock except: Alamy, 16-17; Getty, 8-9, 12-13, 21; Thinkstock, 18-19, 20.

Printed in the United States of America at Corporate Graphics in North Mankato, Minnesota.

TABLE OF CONTENTS

CHAPTER 1

GROWING
FRUIT

What do apples
and strawberries
have in common?

Both have seeds.
Both are sweet.

Both are fruit!

The best time to plant fruit depends on where you live.

A good time to plant is in the spring.

Most fruits need at least six hours of full sun each day. They need good **air circulation**.

Choose a spot that's not too windy. Too much wind can blow fruit off the plants. It can keep useful insects like bees away.

DID YOU KNOW?

Fruit is the part of a plant that holds the seeds. You may think that peas and peppers are vegetables. But they are actually fruit! Because they are not sweet, we think of them as vegetables. What other "vegetables" are actually fruit?

Do you know what fruits you want to plant? If so, you need to find out how much sun and space your plants need to grow.

If you have a lot of space, you can plant fruit trees.

CHAPTER 2

TREES AND BERRIES

Most gardeners plant young fruit trees that are already in pots.

Fruit trees need a lot of sun. The soil must have good **drainage**. If the soil holds too much water, the roots can rot.

In late winter or early spring, you need to **prune** fruit trees.

Pruning helps a tree get more sun and grow more fruit. **Mulch** will help keep weeds and **pests** away. Most fruit trees bear fruit three to four years after you plant them.

DID YOU KNOW?

Many fruit trees such as plums and peaches need the cold winter to make spring flowers. The flowers turn into fruit!

If you don't have much space, you can plant **dwarf trees**. These smaller trees are easier to prune. They will give fruit faster.

Berries also don't need a lot of space, and they are easy to grow.

DID YOU KNOW?

Watermelons need a lot of space. They grow on a vine that spreads out along the ground. They do well in places where there is a lot of sun and the nights are warm.

Berries need a lot of sun. Water the plants when they need it. Adding **compost** to well-drained soil will help them grow.

You will want to protect your plants from pests like slugs and beetles.

If you can, plant berries in a place where you can look at them every day. This will help you see pests quickly so you can remove them.

slug

CHAPTER 3

HARVESTING FRUIT

You will **harvest** most fruit from mid-summer through the fall. How do you know when your fruit is ready?

Most fruit is ripe when its color is bright and it smells sweet. You can eat it right away. Or you use it to make something else, like jam! How do you eat your fruit?

ACTIVITIES & TOOLS

GROW YOUR OWN STRAWBERRIES

You don't need a lot of space to grow your own strawberries. You can grow them in a pot in a sunny window. Here's how:

What You Need:

- young strawberry plant (You can purchase one online or from your local garden shop or transplant one from another garden.)
- gravel
- garden soil
- pot

1. Put a layer of gravel about a half inch (1.3 centimeters) deep in a pot. This will give the soil good drainage.

2. Put a little soil in the pot. Push the soil away toward the edges of the pot to create a hole in the center.

3. Add a small mound of soil in the middle of the hole.

4. Lower the plant into the pot. Set the plant on the mound in the center of the hole. Fan the roots down the side of the mound.

5. Fill in the hole with soil. Then fill the pot up to the base of the plant's stem. Pat the soil down.

6. Make sure the plant stays moist and gets plenty of sun.

7. Keep it up! In three months you should have berries!

GLOSSARY

air circulation: The movement of air.

compost: A rotted mix of leaves, grass, and paper that makes garden soil healthier.

drainage: A way to get rid of extra water.

dwarf trees: A smaller form of a larger tree.

harvest: The time for gathering fruits, vegetables, or flowers.

mulch: Dead leaves or wood chips that you spread around a plant to control weeds.

pests: Insects, animals, or other plants than can hurt growing plants.

prune: To cut off the parts of a plant that are not wanted.

INDEX

TO LEARN MORE

Learning more is as easy as 1, 2, 3.

1) Go to www.factsurfer.com

2) Enter "fruits" into the search box.

3) Click the "Surf" to see a list of websites.

With factsurfer, finding more information is just a click away.